TRANSITIONS RESOURCE

Divorce Support Group

RECOVER / DISCOVER WORKBOOK

Transitions Resource Divorce Support Group
RECOVER / DISCOVER AGENDA

Session 1:   Welcome and Introductions

The Benefits of a Structured Support Group

Court and Therapy/Support Groups are not the same

Pledge of Participation and Healing/ Participant Guidelines

Homework: My Personal Profile through Item 3 "Frightened and Scared"

Session 2:   Grieving the Change-Frightened and Scared

Pledge

Open discussion of Item 3 only "Frightened and Scared"

Group exercise –Creative Visualization & Self Talk

Homework: "Angry and Mad"

Session 3:   Grieving the Change-Angry and Mad

Pledge

Open discussion of "Angry and Mad"

Group exercise -Safe Techniques to Process Anger

Homework: "Sad or Depressed"

Session 4:   Grieving the Change-Sad and Depressed

Pledge

Open discussion "Sad or Depressed"

Group exercise-Putting Pain Away

Homework: "Acceptance"

Session 5:   Grieving the Change-Accepting Your Present

Pledge

Open discussion "Acceptance"

Group exercise –Changing Your Story/Positive Affirmations

Homework: "Hope and Joy"

Session 6:   Grieving the Change-Hope and Joy

Pledge

Open discussion "Hope and Joy"

Group exercise – Freedom of Forgiveness

Homework: Strengthen Your Beliefs for Hope and Discover Workbook pages 1-12

Session 7:   Strengthen Your Beliefs for Hope

Pledge

Open Discussion: Develop Your Beliefs for Hope

Group Exercise: Benefits of Beliefs, Identify Personal Blocks

Homework: Be Grateful in Adversity and Discover workbook pages 13-25

Session 8:   Be Grateful in Adversity

Pledge

Open Discussion: Living Gratefully Minded

Group exercise-Daily Gratitude Journal

Homework: Think Positive Thoughts and Discover workbook pages 27-39

Session 9:   Think Positive Thoughts

Pledge

Open discussion: The Thought Habit, Choosing the Right Thoughts

Group exercise –Turning a Wrong Thought into a Right Thought

Homework: Speak Positive Words and Discover workbook pages 40-48

Session 10:   Speak Positive Words

Pledge

Open discussion: The Word Habit, Speaking Gratitude Daily

Group exercise-Turning a Wrong Word into a Right Word

Homework: Reduce Your Worry/Stress/Anxiety and Discover workbook pages 49-58

Session 11:   Reduce Your Worry/Stress/Anxiety

Pledge

Open discussion: Rest and Relaxation

Group exercise-Guided Rest and Guided Meditation

Homework: Discover Your Purpose and Discover workbook pages 59-68

Session 12:   Discover Your Purpose

Pledge

Open discussion: Understand Your Value and Talents, Accepting Your Assignment

Group exercise-Identify Your Purpose

Homework: Live Your Purpose and Discover workbook pages 69-75

Session 13:   Live Your Purpose

Pledge

Open discussion: Living with Purpose

Group exercise-Using What You Have, Practicing Active Listening and Assertive Communication Techniques

Homework: Complete Your Plan of Action and Discover Workbook 76-92

3

RECOVER/DISCOVER

SESSION 1

Welcome and Introductions

The Benefits of a Structured Support Group

If you're facing a major stressful life change, you don't have to go it alone. A support group can help.

Support groups bring together people facing similar issues, whether that's illness, relationship problems or major life changes. Members of support groups often share experiences and advice. It can be helpful just getting to talk with other people who are in the same boat.

While not everyone wants or needs support beyond that offered by family and friends, you may find it helpful to turn to others outside your immediate circle. A support group can help you cope better and feel less isolated as you make connections with others facing similar challenges. A support group shouldn't replace your standard medical care, but it can be a valuable resource to help you cope.

Members of a support group typically share their personal experiences and offer one another emotional comfort and moral support. They may also offer practical advice and tips to help you cope with your situation. Benefits of participating in support groups may include:

- Feeling less lonely, isolated or judged

- Gaining a sense of empowerment and control

- Improving your coping skills and sense of adjustment

- Talking openly and honestly about your feelings

- Reducing distress, depression or anxiety

- Developing a clearer understanding of what to expect with your situation

- Getting practical advice or information about treatment options

- Comparing notes about resources, such as doctors and alternative options

Court and Therapy/Support Groups are NOT the same

The differences between what an Attorney versus Therapist/ Support Groups can provide:

   a. Court isn't for dirty laundry-Therapy/ Support Group is

   b. Court isn't healing- Therapy/Support Group is

c. Court and the State law aren't necessarily fair

   d. Divorce isn't fair

Your Attorney is not your *Therapist, Doctor, Accountant, Buddy or Parent*, they are your *Legal Representative* only, can only help reach financial settlement/parenting plan.

Get what you need from the people that can provide it:

   a. Seek a **Therapist/Support Group** to process feelings, emotions, grief, expectations & rebuilding confidence

   b. Seek a **Doctor** for physical needs

   c. Maintain **Friendships** to keep you busy and occupied

   d. Use **Parents and Family** for unconditional support

   e. Hire an **Attorney** to legally dissolve a socially binding union and end marriage (Attorneys are not trained or equipped to help with emotional aspects)

Recover / Discover Pledge

I pledge to acknowledge, validate and accept the wounding I have experienced.

I have the right and am entitled to these feelings.

I will take the time to grieve and mourn these feelings.

I will take time to study in group and on my own to develop an understanding of the purpose of these wounds and how it will help me grow and serve others.

I understand that clinging to negative thoughts and feelings only hinders my progress in processing my emotions.

I know that I owe myself the privilege to release these feelings and wounds in order to heal and become the hopeful and joyful person I deserve to be.

Participant Guidelines

Confidentiality

This support group is designed to be a safe place to talk openly and share your challenges as well as your successes. It will remain a safe place only if the participants can trust that what is said in the group will not be shared with anyone outside the group.

Participation

While sharing your experience with the group is not required, most participants will experience more healing when they allow others to share their pain, grief and joys. This can only happen if everyone contributes to the group. The "homework" assignments are designed to be discussed at the following session, so completing the homework will be helpful in preparing your contribution and participation in the sessions.

Content of Participation

This structured program is designed to address the wounding and healing specifically related to divorce and your Ex-Spouse. While some participants may be in current relationships, please refrain from discussions of current relationships and share those experiences relating to your divorce, family and Ex-Spouse only.

Attendance

Participants are encouraged to make every effort to attend all of the sessions. The structured content is accumulative and is designed to work toward a healing outcome. Even if you feel the topic of a given week may not apply to you, your participation is a part of others healing and the entire group can gain from all experiences shared. We ask that you commit to attending as many sessions as possible.

Materials Needed

Participants need their own _Transitions Resource Recover/Discover Workbook and DiscoverYourself Workbook-by Dr. Jessica Blalock, Ph.D._ in order to personalize and journal their experience to gain the most benefit from the program. Participants can purchase the workbooks on Create Space.com.

RECOVER/DISCOVER

SESSION 2

Grieving the Change-Frightened and Scared

MY PERSONAL PROFILE

1.   a. How long was my marriage_____

Minor Children Names/Ages_____

b. Any previous marriages_____

Related children to previous marriages_____

b. Where do I feel I am in the grieving process: (circle one)

Shock   Denial   Despair   Anger   Guilt   Bargaining   Acceptance   Forgiveness

c. How important is marriage or a partner to my self-concept (Scale 1-10)

10 very important   9   8   7   6   5   4   3   2   1 not important

d. What perceptions do I have regarding marriage in general? (my long term dreams of marriage)

1.

2.

3.

4.

5.

2. a. I recollect most often the__ positive or__ negative aspects of marriage? recollections:

1.

2.

3.

4.

My own contributions to the status of the marriage?

1.

2.

3.

3. Emotions: Fill in the blank for all that apply: *Frightened or Scared:*

I feel
 rejected because_____

confused because_____

helpless because_____

powerless because_____

submissive because_____

insecure because_____

anxious because_____

embarrassed because_____

discouraged because_____

insignificant because_____

weak because_____

foolish because_____

Session 2 Group Exercise

When we feel frightened, scared or anxious, self talk and creative visualization can also be tools to calm us and help us feel safe.

Creative Visualization:

Close your eyes and imagine in your mind a place that brings you comfort, warmth, safety and joy. For some this is a favorite vacation spot, a good memory of a childhood home, a special room or environment that one has visited that has brought them joy and peace. An example might be sitting in your favorite beach chair under a shaded umbrella, listening to the ocean roll in. Allow your senses to feel this place completely, feel the warmth of the sun, the breeze through your hair, smell the salty ocean air, see the tide gently rolling in and out in a calming rhythmic motion. Now add the calming self talk.

Self Talk:

Self talk is positive soothing words to speak to yourself either silently in your thoughts or out loud. Some examples would be:

"Everything is fine in the here and now"

"I am safe, I am calm, I am relaxed"

"All is well, All is well"

"This feeling will pass"

As you visualize your safe place, repeat your preferred self-talk phrase over and over again until you have achieved a calm state.

RECOVER/DISCOVER

SESSION 3

Grieving the Change-Angry and Mad

Angry or Mad:

I feel:

hostile because_____

angry because_____

hateful because_____

critical because_____

jealous because_____

selfish because_____

frustrated because_____

furious because_____

irritated because_____

skeptical because_____

Session 3 Group Exercise

Safe Techniques to Process Anger

Pent-up anger can cause a variety of emotional and physical problems if not expressed and processed properly. Anger is a normal emotion experienced during the grieving process of change. Here are some healthy, safe techniques to physically express your anger to bring unhealthy emotions to the surface, process and heal from your pain. Take the time each day or at least several times per week to use these techniques to process your anger and pain regardless if you don't feel angry. This will help you avoid damaging long-term physical symptoms of anger and help you heal more swiftly.

Wet Towel in the Tub

Take a large bath towel and *lightly* dampen it with water to give it weight (do not saturate it). Stand in a bathtub, holding the towel draped behind you with both hands on either end, bring the towel up over your head and down in front of your body, hitting the towel on the tub simultaneously grunting or yelling out loud OR you may express angry words…such as "why did you hurt me?", "I hate that __", "I am angry that ____".

Racquet on the Sofa

Take a sturdy racquet (tennis, racquetball) and pile sofa cushions/pillows on top of each other to a waist high height. Using the same method above, bring the racquet over your head and down onto the cushions simultaneously expressing your anger out loud.

Ice Cubes at a Tree

Take a tray of ice cubes outside and find a tree away from the house with a fairly large trunk. Stand several yards away from the tree and throw ice cubes one at a time at the tree expressing your anger out loud with each one.

These activities may result in tears, this is ok. Allow yourself to feel your anger and express your anger. Crying is a natural release for anger and pain, allow yourself the healing process of tears, you deserve to mourn and express your pain.

RECOVER/DISCOVER

SESSION 4

Grieving the Change-Sad and Depressed

Sad or Depressed:

I feel

sleepy because_____

bored because_____

lonely because_____

depressed because _____

ashamed because_____

guilty because_____

bashful because_____

stupid because_____

miserable because_____

inadequate because_____

inferior because_____

apathetic because_____

b. If I feel betrayed, then by whom? Partner   Self   God   Family   Friends   Employer

4. What is my level of acceptance about breakdown of relationship as I had planned, hoped, dreamed, expected?

Session 4 Group Exercise

Excerpt from Deceived-Claudia Black

"It is usually early in the recovery process that the pain seems overwhelming, but it will pass if you are willing to identify and own it. Feelings are transitory; they pass. As intense as your pain can be, trying to control and defend against your feelings prolongs the pain. Allow yourself to own them and be with them. A lot of what you are experiencing is the accumulation of many years of unacknowledged feelings related to loss and grief.

How long will it hurt? You will experience a wider range and greater depth of feelings as you feel safer. Your pain is both deep and wide. It lessens as you own your pain, shame and anger. You need to live with your pain, accept its' reality and practice healthy behavior until the hurt begins to ease. It may be helpful to think of grief as a hurricane-force wind. If you stand rigid and lock your knees, the wind will surely blow you over. Conversely if you stand and face the wind with balance and flexibility, leaning into it, you may sway like a palm tree, but you will find your strength and durability. Peace comes by walking *through* the pain, not around it. The process of grieving and attending to your losses will take months, and you will periodically find yourself back in the grief process when a specific issue is triggered-even years into your recovery journey. The depth and span of your suffering is strongly influenced by the degree of grief you allow yourself to experience in early recovery.

Freeing yourself from the mental frenzy. One of the biggest challenges grieving partners face is preoccupation and ruminating thoughts. Ruminating is a cognitive attempt to control the situation and to avoid the overwhelming emotions of the situation at a time when you are trying to make sense of it. This mental vigilance is a form of traumatizing yourself. You can be so consumed in your mind-set of preoccupation and rumination that it feels as if you are going crazy with the various images. To get out of your head requires a willingness to recognize that you are the one keeping yourself trapped in this mental frenzy. It begins by accepting that preoccupation doesn't help your situation and only keeps you trapped in defeated thinking."

Accept that you are powerless over other people, places and things but remember that you are NOT powerless over your actions in your recovery. In order to redirect your focus answer the following questions on slips of paper:

What thoughts/visions are the most painful to me?_____

In what ways do I try to control my ex partner?_____

What can I do about this right now to free myself?_____

What action can I take?_____

What decision can I make?_____

Place these slips of paper in a box, label the box "Worry Box" and put the box away in a closet or up on a shelf. Continue to add to the box any unhealthy ruminating thoughts that hinder your healing.

RECOVER/DISCOVER

SESSION 5

Grieving the Change-Acceptance

Emotions. Fill in the blank for all that apply: *Acceptance*

I feel:

content because_____

 thoughtful because_____

intimate because_____

loving because_____

trusting because _____

nurturing because_____

pensive because_____

relaxed because_____

responsive because_____

serene because_____

sentimental because_____

thankful because_____

compassionate because _____

     b. Define my idea of being fair and my Ex partner's idea of fair:

     My idea:

     My Ex Partner's idea:

     c. Do I expect my Ex partner will be "fair" moving forward?

     d. What do I predict to be the main areas of conflict regarding my Ex partner moving forward?

Specifically identify my value system by ranking the following items in order of importance:

Work, religion, family, extracurricular activities/hobbies

Specifically identify my Ex partner's value system in order of importance:

Identify similarities and differences and if I have violated my own value system in the events leading to divorce:

Current Life as I know it is ending, but it begins a new hopeful, improving, happy and healthier status than unhappily married. My current status of hope is:

10 very hopeful   9   8   7   6   5   4   3   2   1 hopeless

Session 5 Group Exercise

Motivational speaker Iyanla Vanzant recognizes that we can become addicted to our painful story of our past and encourages us to "get unstuck from our story" in 3 simple steps.

One: Look at how you contribute to your pain, tell yourself the TRUTH:
Who are you?
What do you want?
What are you willing to do to get it?
What are you not willing to do to get it?
State facts, speak the truth

Two: Ask for what you want. Be willing to get a "NO" answer but know how you will respond to this "no" answer

Three: Get a vision of what you want and put an action plan in place to achieve it

Example:
One:
I am a divorced widow, my children lost their father
I want to be a healthy role-model for my children, show them how to grieve and heal
I want to restore peace, love and joy to our home and environment
I am willing to seek Counseling for self and children
I am not willing to let this event make my children bitter, angry or unhealthy

Two:
Positive Affirmations: I am happy, healthy and joyful; my children are happy, healthy and joyful

Three:
We will tell jokes at the dinner table every night (make sure we laugh every day)
We will share stories daily of one thing that brought us joy that day
We will share a reading or anecdote daily that depicts hope/endurance through difficult times

Choose 5-10 positive affirmations, list them on a note card and read them daily. A list of sample verses and positive affirmations are on the following page.

Sample Positive Affirmations

Every day in every way I'm getting better and better

Everything is coming to me easily and effortlessly

I am a radiant being, filled with light and love

My life is blossoming in total perfection

I am the master of my life

Everything I need is within my reach

I love to love and be loved

The more I love myself, the more love I have to give others

I am now attracting happy relationships into my life

I am always in the right place, at the right time, successfully engaged in the right activity

This is a rich universe and there is plenty for all of us

The more I give, the more I receive and the happier I feel

It's okay for me to have fun and enjoy myself, and I do

I feel happy and blissful

I am open to receiving all the blessings of this abundant universe

I am attractive and lovable

I am kind, loving and have a great deal to share with others

I deserve the best in life

I am willing to be happy and successful

Acceptance

Acceptance is the final stage of grief and loss and is necessary to move through difficult feelings and situations into purposeful forward action. The other stages of grief are denial anger bargaining and sadness. In many situations people stay in the bargaining stage because the sadness seems overwhelming. Bargaining is trying to manipulate the situation to be what you want it to be or trying to make sense of it when there may be no sense to be made.

A good analogy of moving to acceptance is this scenario: If you woke up in the night and your kitchen was ABLAZE on fire, past the point of a bucket of water or fire extinguisher, what would you do? Certainly you would be grieving; grieving the idea of a good night's sleep, grieving the idea of safety in your home, grieving the loss of your kitchen and possibly your house. But if you were stuck in the bargaining stage you would stand on the edge of the fire saying things like, "Why is the kitchen on fire?", "The kitchen should NOT be on fire!", "If I were the kitchen I wouldn't be on fire!", "I am not moving from this spot until we figure out WHY the kitchen is on fire!". All of that sounds pretty ridiculous, doesn't it? To stand stagnant on the edge of a fire asking questions that don't change that the kitchen is indeed ON FIRE. If you didn't move from that spot you would burn up! Yet that's what we do in bargaining, we ask why and say how it should be rather than accepting that things are the way they are and all the why's and should's in the world won't change that.

Acceptance doesn't mean we are happy about the situation or that we are comfortable with it or that we don't try to change our involvement. It just means we accept that it is what it is. The kitchen is on fire, accept it, get out of the house, and call the fire dept. You cannot properly deal with a situation until you call it for what it is. If you are unsure of what it is, look at the history, track record, and probability. If you want your spouse to change, for example, look at their history of change and ask yourself how strong of a probability is it that this time will ACTUALLY be different? Ten percent? Twenty? Fifty? Five? You make the call on what's acceptable and how you will determine your boundaries. But remember, why's and should's will keep you stuck from moving forward. **Just get out of the kitchen!!**

24

RECOVER/DISCOVER

SESSION 6

Grieving the Change-Hope and Joy

Emotions: Fill in the blank to all that apply   *Hope:*

I feel:

proud because_____

respected because_____

appreciated because_____

hopeful because_____

important because_____

faithful because_____

cheerful because_____

satisfied because_____

valuable because_____

worthwhile because_____

intelligent because_____

confident because_____

forgiving because_____

Joy:

I feel:

excited because_____

daring because_____

energetic because_____

playful because_____

creative because_____

aware because_____

delightful because_____

extravagant because_____

amused because_____

stimulating because_____

fascinating because_____

Session 6 Group Exercise

Excerpt from **Deceived**-Claudia Black

"Forgiveness and recovery: The process of true forgiveness begins with acknowledging that a wrong has been done to you. Then you can grieve and own the feelings associated with those wrongs, your pain and anger. Even though the relationship is over, the act of forgiving is about your own healing; about letting go of resentments, preoccupations, and controlling behavior. Ultimately forgiveness is remembering and letting go. It is about being true to you and your higher self. Forgiveness is made possible with your commitment to your own recovery practices.

When you forgive, you no longer build an identity around something that happened to you. You realize that there is more to you than your history with your partner. You recognize that you no longer need your grudges, resentment, hatred or self-pity. You commit to changing your story for the present, the here and now. You don't need these negative emotions as excuses for getting less out of life than you want or deserve. You no longer want to punish the people who hurt you. Forgiveness is the inner peace you feel when you stop trying to do so."

Many people of faith choose to place the fate of those who hurt them in the hands of their higher power and free themselves from "righting the wrong" done to them. This allows them the ability to forgive, knowing that it is not their responsibility to settle the score.

Regarding faith as a means to survive devastatingly painful circumstances, Leslie Dinkins, LCSW, Domestic Violence Victim Counselor states "Of all the victims I have counseled, the majority of those who have emotionally survived and thrived are those that have a strong spiritual faith they rely on for hope and healing."

If not faith, those that rely on the old adage "Everything happens for a reason, and what am I supposed to learn and grow from this experience?" will identify their means to forgiveness.

Today I will forgive _____ for _____

Today I will forgive _____ for _____

Today I will forgive _____ for _____

Today I will forgive _____ for _____

Today I will forgive _____ for _____

RECOVER/DISCOVER

SESSION 7

Strengthen Your Beliefs for Hope

Strengthen Your Beliefs for Hope

It has been said that those who have a positive attitude about expecting good outcomes in the face of a crisis attract positive things into their life that ultimately turn the situation around. We have already addressed how damaging living in your past can be and can hinder you from opening the pipeline for good things to come. If we commit to freeing ourselves from our past and focusing on today and the future instead, our only alternative is to have a positive attitude regarding the unknown of what unfolds today, tomorrow and so on. Take a moment to reflect on an experience you have had where you or someone close to you were optimistic about possible outcomes and they materialized.

Explain this experience to share with the group

_____

_____

_____

_____

_____

_____

_____

_____

_____

_____

_____

_____

29

Develop Your Faith in A Higher Power

To paraphrase, in *The Purpose Driven Life,* Rick Warren teaches: The heart of developing your faith is worship and the heart of worship is surrender. Surrendering to your Higher Power is the heart of worship. It is the natural response to amazing love and mercy. We turn ourselves over, not out of fear or duty, but in love. However there are 3 barriers that block our total surrender to our Higher Power, and they are *Fear, Pride and Confusion.*

Fear keeps us from surrendering, but love casts out all fear. The more we realize how much we are loved, the easier the surrender becomes.

Pride keeps us from surrendering because we don't want to admit that we're just creatures and not in charge of everything, that we cannot control our fate. We still try to give orders and interfere with the Higher Power's work within us.

Confusion keeps us from surrendering because we misunderstand the outcome of surrender. We relate surrender to being passive, a doormat, a coward, losing who we are.

The more we let the Higher Power take us over, the more truly authentic selves we become.

Signs that we know we have truly surrendered: we fully trust. We know we have fully surrendered (end developed our enduring faith) when we rely on our Higher Power consistently to work things out instead of trying to manipulate others, force our own agenda and try to control the situation, we consistently let go and let the Higher Power do the work.

Benefits of fully surrendering: We experience peace, freedom (a freedom felt like never before) and experience the miraculous power of the Higher Power's work in our life.

Sometimes it takes years, but eventually we discover that the greatest hindrance to blessings in our lives is not others, but our own selves. Our self will, stubborn pride, personal ambition, own plans for ourselves that block our Higher Power from doing His best work on us. So give it all: our past regrets, our present problems, our future ambitions, our fears, our dreams, our weaknesses, bad habits, hurts and hang-ups. Hand it over and put your Higher Power in the driver's seat and take our hands off the wheel."

List your personal blocks that are hindering positive blessings in your life:

Past regrets_____

Present problems_____

Fears_____

Weaknesses_____

Bad Habits_____

Hurts_____

Future Ambitions_____

Dreams_____

RECOVER/DISCOVER

SESSION 8

Be Grateful in Adversity

Be Grateful In Adversity

In order to completely move past our pain, not only do we need to be grateful for the good things, but also for the adversarial things that life throws at us. When you adjust your perspective to acknowledge and see the "silver lining around every dark cloud" you are developing your faith in anticipation that there is a purpose, growth and a lesson in every experience that we have. In fact our challenges and suffering tests us and helps us to develop our character. The characteristics these adversities are intended to develop are: patience, courage, forgiveness, compassion, integrity and faith.

Rick Warren observes:

> Your most profound and intimate experiences of faith will likely be in your darkest days-when your heart is broken, when you feel abandoned, when you are out of options, when the pain is the greatest-and you turn to your faith.

> Every problem is a character-building opportunity, and the more difficult it is, the greater the potential for building spiritual muscle and moral fiber.

> In these times of trouble, we need to continually remind ourselves that the overall plan for us has yet to be revealed, but that it is a good plan.

While it may seem difficult in the height of crisis or heartache, it is important to acknowledge our blessings daily. If we cannot do this with the big things we are struggling with, we can at least start with the little things, something as simple as a pretty blue sky, the fact that we have our daily provisions; shelter over our heads, clothes on our back, food on our table.

The most powerful way to become gratefully-minded for our adversity is to acknowledge that our Higher Power's timing is not always our timing. Accept that we cannot understand at this time however, also accept that at some point the blessings in store will be revealed for what we have endured and that all of the suffering and heartache has a much bigger purpose and is a means to an end that we cannot see or even fathom at this time.

Session 8 Group Exercise

Take a personal inventory of your adversities, how you will grow from them and the blessings in your life today

Adversities and Challenges

1)_____
_____
2)_____
_____
3)_____
_____
4)_____
_____
5)_____
_____
6)_____
_____
7)_____
_____
8)_____

What characteristic will this help me develop:

Patience, courage, forgiveness, compassion, integrity, faith

1)_____
_____
2)_____
_____
3)_____
_____
4)_____
_____
5)_____
_____
6)_____
_____
7)_____
_____
8)_____

I am grateful and blessed in the following areas because:

Family_____

Friends_____

Employment_____

Small daily observations of blessings:

Monday_____

Tuesday_____

Wednesday_____

Thursday_____

Friday_____

Saturday_____

Sunday_____

RECOVER/DISCOVER

SESSION 9

Think Positive Thoughts

Think Positive Thoughts

We have already explored the benefits of positive affirmations. In _Making Good Habits_ Joyce Meyer explains:

"When you are trying to develop a good habit or break a bad one, always remember that thoughts precede words, words precede action. Or, as I frequently say, "Where the mind goes, the man follows." We must learn to think what we truly want, not what we feel, or even what we currently have. We can literally talk ourselves into victory or defeat. Don't ever settle for anything less than the best. This is one of the main reasons we need the positive thought/positive word habit. You can rid yourself of any unpleasant thought by simply deciding to think something else. Positive affirmations help in this process. Take responsibility for your thoughts and begin choosing them carefully because they are the raw material for your words and actions.

In _The Anxiety Cure,_ Dr. Archibald Hart explains that in order to change our thinking habits, first we have to "capture" our thoughts rushing through our mind before we can change them. He shares a 3 step strategy to changing our thinking habits:
"
      1) slow down your thinking
      2) challenge your mistaken beliefs
      3) speak the truth to yourself

Slow down your thinking and try to move them from a subconscious state to a conscious state, be aware of your thoughts rather than just letting them flow.

Challenge your mistaken beliefs by getting yourself a little notebook to record your beliefs whenever you catch them. Date the page. Throughout the day try to capture and record thoughts that imply beliefs that may be mistaken. Then write down your challenge of that mistaken belief. As an example:
    Mistaken Belief: I am the victim of the way others have treated me.
    Challenge: Nonsense, I can take control of my life now and change the outcome.
    Mistaken Belief: People should always love and respect me.
    Challenge: Who says? People respond to me in the way I treat them. If I want respect, I must show respect.
    Mistaken Belief: I am just the way I am, I can't change
    Challenge: Not true, the gospel is all about change, it may not be easy but everyone can change.

Speak the truth to yourself by establishing a set of well-rehearsed self-statements you can draw on when you need to counter an unhealthy thought. These need to be rehearsed frequently so that they spring to mind when you need them, so write them down and take the time to memorize them. Here are some samples, but add some of your own that will be most effective for you:

I don't need to fight my feelings, they only last a short time, then they go away
I am going to focus my thoughts away from my hurtful feelings
So I feel some hurt (pain) right now, so what, everyone feels hurt (pain) some time or other
I am going to be alright in a short while, so I will think about something else and continue what I'm doing
Heartbreak (or pain) is as old as time, I don't have to allow it to control me, I can control it
Right now I am having feelings I don't like, but I know how to treat them so that they will go away
This seems like an impossible situation right now, but I won't feel helpless, I'll move forward with courage
I can control my feelings, I choose to overlook them and focus on other things
Feelings are only phantoms-they exist only if I allow them to"

Session 9 Group Exercise

Review Session 4 Healing Exercise "Free yourself from the mental frenzy" paragraph.

List your top 5 Mistaken Beliefs

1)_____
2)_____
3)_____
4)_____
5)_____

List Your Challenges that correlate to your top 5 Mistaken Beliefs by number

1)_____
2)_____
3)_____
4)_____
5)_____

List your Top 5 Truths that you want to memorize

1)_____
2)_____
3)_____
4)_____
5)_____

Have each participant share their top 2 in each category.

RECOVER/DISCOVER

SESSION 10

Speak Positive Words

Speak Positive Words

We have studied how your thoughts can determine your words, your words can determine your actions. What you say out loud in the midst of your challenge has a lasting impact on how long you stay in those situations. When you continually speak of how wronged you have been or how hurt and unhappy your are, you will continually remain in the downtrodden or victim mindset, however when you speak of how blessed, happy, joyful, healed you are, you are preparing yourself for a hopeful, joyful future.

If it is too difficult to speak of your blessings just yet, then try to focus on speaking about your enduring faith that will bring about a joyful future.

Watch your thoughts, for they become words.
Watch your words, for they become actions.
Watch your actions, for they become habits.
Watch your habits, for they become character.
Watch your character, for it becomes your destiny.

Session 10 Group Exercise

Write 5 Affirmations on a 3 X 5 note card and commit to reading them out loud to yourself daily or multiple times per day. Some individuals like to tape these to their bathroom mirrors so that they see them first thing in the morning, last thing in the evening. Have the group share their top 2 from their note cards.

RECOVER/DISCOVER

SESSION 11

Reduce Your Worry/Stress/Anxiety

Reduce Your Worry, Stress and Anxiety

In *The Anxiety Cure,* Dr. Archibald Hart prescribes:

"Time for rest must be taken on a daily basis and should never be delayed longer than a week. It is the principle of a Sabbath that I think we need to observe. It is more than observing one day of rest. Every day needs its hours of rest (a good night's sleep for example). And every week needs its day of rest (for development of faith). Ways you can maintain this principle are:
1) Pay careful attention to developing an awareness of your limits.
2) Never work until you have reached your limits.
3) The moment you realize you are approaching your limits, stop.
4) Maintain regular breaks during your workday.
5) If you exceed your limits and find yourself in stress or pain, back off and allow time for recovery.
6) Take a good rest at the end of every day.
7) Take a good rest on weekends.

What is rest? Rest is not catching up on activities or participating in hobbies. What characterizes rest is that it is not an activity. It is pure, luxurious leisure, a time to rediscover yourself, catch up on your feelings, determine your new priorities, recreate a sense of balance, restore your soul.

Resting is not the same as relaxing. We need to learn how to rest as well as relax. Relaxation involves turning off both your mind and your muscles. Relaxation lowers your stress hormones, including adrenaline and the "sad messengers" like cortisol. It elevates your immune system, raises your tolerance for pain, increases your natural tranquilizers, allows damaged tissue to repair itself and helps your body rejuvenate itself. So how does one relax? The basic ingredients in all relaxation include:
1) sit or lie in a comfortable position
2) ensure you won't be interrupted
3) set aside a predetermined amount of time for the exercise (30-45 minutes is ideal)
4) don't fall asleep
5) remain inactive (don't fidget, move, get up or scratch)
6) avoid thinking troublesome thoughts

One form of relaxation is Meditation. In *The Daily Habit of These Outrageously Successful People* (The Huffington Post-7/5/13) Carolyn Gregoire quotes the following from our mentors and most successful business leaders:

"Meditation more than anything in my life was the biggest ingredient of whatever success I've had." Ray Dalio, Billionaire Founder of Bridgewater Associates

Ford Motor Company Chairman Bill Ford and former Google.org Director Larry Brilliant are also among the executives advocating the mindfulness practice.

New Corp CEO Rupert Murdock recently tweeted that he was trying out Transcendental Meditation: Everyone recommends, not that easy to get started, but said to improve everything!"

The Ford Motor Company Chairman is a big proponent of meditation in the business world, according to Inc. Magazine, at this year's Wisdom 2.0 Conference, Ford was interviewed by leading American Buddhist teacher Jack Kornfield and stated that during difficult times at the company, he set an intention every morning to go through his day with compassion, to lead with compassion. Ford said he first learned to develop compassion for himself thorough a loving-kindness meditation practice.

An outspoken advocate of TM, Oprah has said she sits in stillness for 20 minutes twice daily. After a meditation session in Iowa last year she said "I walked away feeling fuller than when I'd come in. Full of hope, a sense of contentment and deep joy. Knowing for sure that even in the daily craziness that bombards us from every direction, there is—still—the constancy of stillness. Only from that space can you create your best work and your best life."

Hip-hop mogul Russell Simmons has long practiced TM meditation speaking out about the benefits of the practice and resides on the board of advisors for the David Lynch Foundation for Consciousness-Based Education and World Peace.

Arianna Huffington described early-morning yoga and meditation as two of her "joy-triggers", now she has brought meditation into her company offering weekly classes to her employees. "Stress-reduction and mindfulness don't just make us happier and healthier, they're a proven competitive advantage for any business that wants one she recently wrote in a blog.

In order to meditate there are two essential ingredients you need to focus on as you develop your ability to practice meditation. First-develop an ability to focus on something specific and second- get into the habit of practicing on a regular basis.

Each day I will commit to rest by:

_____

_____

Each week I will commit to rest by:

_____

_____

My preferred method of relaxation and mediation is:

_____

_____

Depending on your preferred method list the visuals, images, affirmations or mantra's you will focus on during meditation:

_____

_____

Session 11 Group Exercise

Exercise in Rest

Facilitator will lead the group by reading the following activity, dim the lights if possible, set a silent timer to go off in 25 minutes. Read to group in a soft, soothing tone of voice.

"Make yourself comfortable, uncross your legs, arms, remove shoes and glasses, lay flat on your back and close your eyes.

Clear your mind of worries or resentments. Claim peace and tranquility for yourself.

Raise your hands above your head and rest them, don't grasp anything. Take a deep breath, hold it for a few seconds, relax and breathe out.

Now stretch your hands up as far as they will go, farther, hold them there

Now push your feet down as far as they will go, farther, hold them there

Count slowly to 10 silently in your mind as I count to 10 aloud

1...2...3...4...5...6...7....8...9...10

Relax and let your hands and feet return to their original position

Count slowly to 10 silently in your mind as I count to 10 aloud

1...2...3...4...5...6...7....8...9...10

(repeat the stretch, count to 10, then repeat the relax, count to ten once more)

Breathe in and out slowly, rhythmically for a few minutes (4-5 minutes silently)

Remain immobile, resting and relaxing. Don't worry, I will mind the time

(When the timer goes off)

When you are ready, open your eyes, be aware of your body awakening, sit up slowly, moving slowly and peacefully, get up slowly"

Exercise in Meditation- Self-Love

Facilitator will lead the group by reading the following activity, dim the lights if possible, set a silent timer to go off in 25 minutes and read the following in a soft, soothing tone of voice

Sit comfortably, remove shoes, glasses, rest your arms , hands palms up in your lap, close your eyes.

Breathe in and out, slowly, concentrating on listening to the sound of your breath

Relax and quiet your mind. Our mantra today will be " *I am love* " you may visualize the words or an image of your interpretation of the mantra.

Today we will set our intentions of finding and expanding self-love in our physical and energetic bodies

Consider who you are.

Visualize yourself and the joy and wonderment you have brought to others, your parents, your siblings, your children, friends, co-workers, even strangers. Invite them into your space and ask that they connect with you

Love what you have brought them

Appreciate how the special you was just what they needed in so many instances

Absorb the love they feel for you

Visualize that now I am love

Know now how it is that you came to be you in this time and place

Be still with that, it is perfection, it is pure, it is joy, it is love

People love you, people need you, people express love to you, you are a good person, forgive yourself for your mistakes. Mistakes are simply part of life, give them no emotion, definition or rationale, simply observe them and let them go away

Love yourself for experiencing mistakes

Visualize the joy and wonderment you have brought to the earths' creatures, love that sharing, hold it as a precious gift.

Be still with that, It is perfection, It is pure. It is joy.

Now silently focus on the mantra " *I am love* " release all thought except " *I am love* " repeating it over and over again.

Do not worry, I will mind the time, when it is time to release the mantra, you will hear the timer go off.

Remain silent for the remainder of the session until the timer goes off

(When the timer goes off)

It is time to release the mantra " *I am love ..... I am love ...I am love* ".

When you are ready, slowly open your eyes, be aware of your body awakening, sit peacefully until you are ready to get up, get up slowly

RECOVER/DISCOVER

SESSION 12

Discover Your Purpose

Discover Your Purpose

Many believe that it is only through this crisis, most difficult of times are we inspired to dig deep to discover ourselves and our true calling. All of our normal, daily distractions are removed at the height of our wounding and we are open to make sense out of the senselessness of our situation.

In *The Purpose Driven Life,* Rick Warren explains:

" We are not put on earth just to consume resources, but to make a permanent, significant contribution.. Service is the pathway to real significance, how you can make a difference in his world. Work through your crisis, your heartbreak, through YOUR experiences which gives you your own pathway to serve others. These experiences were not given to you for your own benefit, but for the benefit of others, just as others were given experiences that they will share for your benefit.

Many counselors will encourage one who is immobilized with sadness, depression or uncertainty to simply put their emotions aside and do something to help another, to volunteer to help someone or some organization that needs support. The benefits of this gesture are to temporarily take one's mindset off of themselves and dwelling in their present mode and focus on another's needs. This can be a very rewarding experience, something as simple as feeding a neighbor, driving a friend somewhere they need to go, stuffing envelopes for a non-profit organization. The distraction can be very therapeutic.

So, how do we discover how to serve? Warren gives us guidance:

"In determining your area for serving examine these kinds of experiences from your past:

Family experiences: What did you learn growing up in your family?

Educational experiences: What were your favorite subjects in school?

Vocational experiences: What jobs have you been most effective in and enjoyed the most?

Spiritual experiences: What have been your most meaningful times with your spirituality and faith?

Painful experiences: What problems, hurts, thorns and trials have you learned from?

The very experiences you have resented or regretted the most are the ones you have been given to be used to help others! But you must be willing to share them. People are always more encouraged when we share how we survived in our weakest times rather than brag about our strengths. Experience is not what happens to you, it is what you do with that experience that is the key. Don't waste your pain, use it to help others."

Session 12 Group Exercise

Paraphrasing a discussion between Talk Show Host, Oprah Winfrey and Rick Warren, Author of *__A Purpose Driven Life__*:

*The best use of life is love, the best expression of love is time, the best time to love is now. You will find your purpose and your purpose will become significant when you serve others. That's how you raise yourself from acknowledging your purpose and current success to a **significant** life that creates a legacy.*

What experience can I offer to use to serve others?

_____
_____
_____
_____

Identify your likes and dislikes. What are you passionate about? Figure out what you love to do-what you have a heart to do, and then do it.

What are my likes, passions, what do I love to do?

_____
_____
_____

In the next Session we will help devise a plan to merge the two (experiences and likes) to help you find your purpose and put a plan into place that will give you a significant opportunity to make a difference in your life and others.

RECOVER/DISCOVER

SESSION 13

Live Your Purpose

Live Your Purpose

In *The Purpose Driven Life*, Rick Warren gives clear ways to figure out where your purpose to serve will ultimately become clear. He explains that the best way to discover your gifts is to try experimenting with different ways to serve. Don't wait to volunteer until you define your gifts, throw yourself into a variety of ways to serve others and your gifts and talents will emerge when you begin to feel passion about one area or another. Until you start serving, you're not going to know what you are good at. Some ideas he suggests are:

1) Try teaching, leading or organizing for a program or entity
2) Play an instrument or sing
3) Work with teenagers in youth groups, tutoring or mentoring in Big Brother or YMCA or YWCA programs
4) Volunteer free time to a non-profit organization, hospital or elder care facility
5) Serve at a local Food Bank, Homeless Sheltor or Soup Kitchen, or Domestic Violence Advocacy
6) Volunteer in your neighborhood to coordinate or coach youth sports programs
7) Organize or volunteer for a fundraising event for a well-deserving charity
8) Find a group who has similar painful experiences and share your story and testimony

And share your personal story along the way, those who are suffering need your testimony to understand and develop hope for healing. Include the following points when you share your life experiences to help others grow and heal:

What have I learned from failure or heartache?
What have I learned from lack of money or resources?
What have I learned from pain, sorrow or depression?
What have I learned through waiting?
What have I learned through illness?
What have I learned from disappointment?
What have I learned from my family and my relationships?

Be patient with yourself as you try new areas of service. If one area just isn't right for you, try another. When it doesn't work out, don't consider it a failure, consider it an experiment, you will eventually learn what you are good at. You will find that people who don't understand your desire to find and perfect your gift will criticize you and try to get you to conform to what they think you should be doing, but *ignore them!*

Once you have determined your gift and area of service, remember to have the authentic intention to serve. Having the heart of a true servant means serving without expectation

49

of personal gain, being available to serve when the need arises, always looking for those in need and someone to serve, and simply doing what needs to be done. Some of the most glorious opportunities to serve come in the smallest, most discreet of packages. A true servant doesn't need recognition or notoriety for their efforts The most significant service is often the service that is unseen.

So ask yourself, who do I desire to help the most? And get to it!

Which of the above Serving suggestions appeals to me the most? (list in priority of interest)

1)_____

2_____

3)_____

4)_____

When wrapping up the final session of the group, establish an "Accountability follow-up". One month after the last session, circulate an email to the group participants having them report to all what action(s) they have taken to begin to identify their purpose.

Session 13 Group Exercise

Sharing our personal story can be painful but can be most healing when taken from the perspective of how we can use it to help others. Take a moment to consider your experiences and journal below your interpretation of what this taught you. Those courageous enough can share their testimony with the group.

My experience(s) in bullet points:

* _____
* _____
* _____
* _____
* _____
* _____
* _____

Based on these experiences I believe I learned:

from failure or heartache:

_____

from lack of money or resources:

_____

from pain, sorrow or depression

_____

from waiting:

_____

from illness:

_____

from disappointment:

_____

from (fill in your own word) _____:

_____

from (fill in your own word) _____:

_____

What have I learned from my family and my relationships?

_____
_____

51

RESOURCES

Citations and Suggested Additional Readings:

Creative Visualization – Shakti Gawain

Deceived – Claudia Black

Making Good Habits – Joyce Meyer

Peace From Broken Pieces – Iyanla Vanzant

The Anxiety Cure – Dr. Archibald D. Hart

The Purpose Driven Life – Rick Warren

Additional Inspirational Readings:

The Four Agreements – Don Miguel Ruiz

God Calling – A.J. Russell

Jesus Calling – Sarah Young

The Prayer of Jabez – Bruce Wilkinson

You Can Heal Your Life – Louise L. Hay

Forgiving Forward: Unleashing the Forgiveness Revolution – Bruce /Toni Hebel